THE BIG HOUSE ON FLAVIAN

JEMAYNE L. KING

Text Copyright © 2025 by Jemayne King
All rights reserved. This book may not be reproduced or stored in
whole or in part by any means without the written permission
of the author except for brief quotations for the purpose of review.

ISBN: 978-1-966343-74-5 (Hard Cover)
      978-1-966343-75-2 (Soft Cover)

King. Jemayne
The Big House on Flavian

Edited by: Hannah Cohen

Published by Warren Publishing
Charlotte, NC
www.warrenpublishing.net
Printed in the United States

To Paula,
You make me swoon;
you'd even impress Herbert Moon.

For every page ... and every moment in between.

PRAISE FOR *THE BIG HOUSE ON FLAVIAN*

"One of the greatest video games ever made takes on new meaning in this unique collection of poems. The Big House on Flavian *renders the world of* Red Dead Redemption *in literary form, endowing it with new color, emotion, and humanity. For those captivated by the game or those curious about Western history, King's book will be a very enjoyable ride."*

—**Tore Olsson**, author of *Red Dead's History: A Video Game, an Obsession, and America's Violent Past*

"Jemayne L. King has brilliantly woven the threads of a fiction redemptive Western story into a collection of poems that captures our present-day stories of struggles and resiliency. If you are a fellow Red Dead Redemption gunslinger, this book will bring the gaming experience to life and take you on a therapeutic adventure, revealing pieces of yourself, your thoughts, and most of all, your desire to win both the video game and in the game of life!"

— **Chiniqua Radford**, LSATP, LPC; *Radford Real Talk* Podcast; author of *Courage Under Fire: Pocket Therapy to Endure Life's Challenges*

CONTENTS

I. Foundations

A New Future Imagined 3
Ballad of the Robber Baron 4
Veneno Americano 6
Veneno Americano Dos 7
He's Just Gonna Use You, Cremello Gold 8
An Aura of Safety 9
Three Mariners 10
Widow 11
There Will Be a Party 12
Exit, Pursued by a Natural Predator 13
I Didn't Know I Was Talking to a Lady 14
Blessed Are the Piece Makers 15

II. Blood and Dust

A Fisher of Men? 18
Blood Feud 19
Knew Bordeaux 20
The Big House on Flavian 21
I'm Your Huckleberry 22
Ain't No Rules in War, Mister 23
Peeling Mangoes in Tahiti 24
Dictators Fall 25
Last Boy 26
You Don't Hire a Saint to Catch a Sinner 27
Pearson Math 28
Who Are These GD Creeps? 29

III. Law, Loss, and Legacy

Rattus Rattus 33
Legal Work 34
Evolve 35
Call Them Now 36
I'm Happy to Help a Little 37
Open Worlds 38
An Outlaw Shaped By Air and Fire 39
YOU AYE PEE 40
The Green Clan 41
A Crine Man 42
Widow II 43
Red One 44

IV. Redemption and Ruin

I'm Looking for a Discouraged Man 47
Lamb's Heart 48
Godforsaken Money Lender 49
Hereby 50
Saint Denis by Gaslight 51
Naw, He Was Bigger 52
Con Job Drip 53
Beast Fable 54
Mulier Est Ruina Viri 55
Strawberry, 3 a.m. 56
This Game of Ours 57
Boom B.A.P. 1907 58
Arabian or Appaloosa 59
The Greatest Game I've Ever Played 60

The Big House on Flavian is an independent, transformative work inspired by the themes, tone, and narrative structure of *Red Dead Redemption 2*, developed by Rockstar Games. This book is not endorsed by, affiliated with, or associated with Rockstar Games, Take-Two Interactive, or any of their subsidiaries. All trademarks and titles referenced remain the property of their respective owners.

PART I
FOUNDATIONS

A NEW FUTURE IMAGINED

She's got a laugh that breaks like spring
in a town where the trees forgot how to bloom.
Every syllable, soft thunder,
calls back a version of me I thought I buried.
I trace the echo of her voice
like a bootprint through the mud of memory.
Was it always this quiet before,
or did I just learn to hear again?
She's got eyes like pre-war windows,
clear to let all the hope in
but fragile enough to shatter
with one wrong word.
And I–
I am not built for the keeping of joy.
Too many hands taught me to hold with fists.
Too many nights taught me to pray only in retreat.
So I look at her
and I think of safe places,
and I think of leaving them.

BALLAD OF THE ROBBER BARON

He came west not for the land,
but for what lay beneath it–
iron veins and coal-black breath,
tracks to be laid like scripture.
He spoke in ledgers,
wrote sermons in soot.
Towns rose like tombstones
where he struck his claim,
each one carved with a promise
never meant to keep.
He never lifted a hammer,
but a thousand hands broke for him.
Steel bent to his will.
Mules dropped under his watch.
Men vanished into mountains
and came out as ghosts
with gold in their pockets
and blood on their teeth.
He dressed like he knew
God would want to talk business.
In the city, they called him progress.
In the camps, they cursed his name
like a bitter prayer,
choked down with stale whiskey
and the taste of dynamite.
But time does not kneel for empire.
One morning came quiet–
no telegraphs, no trains.
The oil ran dry,
the banks turned their backs,
and the smoke that once crowned him
rose from his own burning office.
He died with clean hands
and no sons to lie for him.

So they called him a builder.
Called him bold.
Named a school,
a street,
a steel bridge in his honor.
But the widows know better.
The land remembers.
And the earth once scarred,
has started to heal
over his name.

VENENO AMERICANO

I walked through fire with a fist full of rage,
Wrote a death wish down on every page.
Got a name, got a face, got a gun to grip,
Got a grudge like a chain 'round my bottom lip.
He killed my kin, so I killed his man,
Then I killed his friend, and I killed his clan.
Every shot rang out like a gospel verse,
But the choir I led only made things worse.
No peace, no sleep, just red in my head,
Even when I prayed, I just talked to the dead.
They told me *"Son, you're becoming what you hate,"*
But I sped through Hell like I couldn't hit the brakes.
See, revenge ain't sweet–it's a poison wine,
It kills real slow, and it lies just fine.
It'll rot your soul while you puff your chest,
Make a grave your bed, and call it rest.
I forgot what love or mercy meant,
Too busy counting every cent of regret.
Now my hands don't shake–they burn,
And every corner I cut takes a darker turn.
Yeah, I got my man, put him in the ground,
But the silence that followed was the loudest sound.
'Cause for every force, there's one the same,
That's Newton's Law–you play, you pay.
So now I ride through the storm I made,
With a heart full of ash and a soul decayed.
My story ends where the snakes all hiss,
Choked by the venom I filled with fists.

VENENO AMERICANO DOS

Caminé entre fuego con rabia en la piel,
escribí mi venganza con tinta y con hiel.
Un nombre, un rostro, un gatillo apretado,
una furia que ruge, un destino sellado.
Mató a mi gente, le maté el compa,
y luego al primo, con fuego y trompa.
Cada bala sonaba como canto sagrado,
pero el coro que guié terminó maldecido y callado.
Sin paz, sin sueño, solo sangre en mi sien,
hasta mis rezos hablaban con los que no ven.
Me dijeron: "*Ya eres lo que odias, hermano,*"
pero seguí matando con puño profano.
La venganza no es dulce–es vino envenenado,
te atrapa despacio y te deja cegado.
Pudre el alma, endurece el pecho,
te acuesta en la tumba como si fuera un lecho.
Olvidé lo que es amar o perdonar,
con los ojos rojos de tanto odiar.
Ahora mis manos no tiemblan: arden,
y cada camino que tomo se parte.
Sí, lo encontré y le puse fin,
pero el silencio gritó: "*Aquí no hay porvenir.*"
Porque toda acción trae reacción,
esa es la ley–la tercera, de Newton.
Ahora cabalgo la tormenta que hice,
con el alma hecha polvo, el corazón que me dice:
"*Tu historia termina donde silban las serpientes,*"
ahogado en el veneno que llevabas en los dientes.

HE'S JUST GONNA USE YOU, CREMELLO GOLD

He shimmers in the light like a crown on the plain,
Cremello Gold glow, no need to explain.
Moves like a whisper, cuts through the breeze,
Dutch Warmblood steppin' with a monarch's ease.
Not just a horse, nah, he's regal with stance,
Even wild mustangs stop, give him a glance.
Sun hit his coat like a verse in a hymn,
You could ride any steed, but he's built to win.
Gallop like thunder, mane all clean,
Trail dust swirl like a sepia dream.
A gift from a soldier, a beast of pride,
You don't ride him—man, you glide.
He's the type to carry legends, not just gear,
When you see that glow, know the end is near.
Eyes like ember, calm but wise,
Came from the storm with the stillest stride.
He don't buck, don't break, don't fold on fate,
Standin' like hope at the outlaw's gate.
Ain't no stable could claim that king,
He's that rare one that shouldn't be sold,
that **vibrant**
majestic
gold-coated thing.

AN AURA OF SAFETY
A modest proposal to stay in Chapter 2

Camp's still humming on the cliffside breeze,
and Strauss is barking 'bout unpaid fees.
Uncle's snoring with beer on his lip.
Don't shake the world, just let it slip.
The stew ain't cold, the nights ain't loud,
and Dutch still dreams aloud and proud.
He's got a plan, and nobody's dead,
the Pinkertons haven't crept in your head.
You got horses to brush, deer to track,
and Hosea's laugh to keep you back.
Micah's mouth ain't ruined the air;
you can pretend he's barely there.
Valentine's muddy and full of sin,
but no one's gone and burned it in.
You can fish with Jack,
Play cards with Sean,
pretend the world won't soon be gone.
'Cause after this? The blood runs thick.
Good men fall, and time moves quick.
You'll ride through storms and things will break,
and every promise Dutch makes? Fake.
So stay awhile, ye gallant fool,
splash in the creek, let the fire cool.
Don't press "next." Don't ride ahead.
Let the future mourn the dead.
Right here, the air still tastes like pine,
and nothing costs you your peace of mind.
So roll another smoke and pass the flask.
Chapter Two is heaven.
Don't ask.

THREE MARINERS

Three mariners at dawn's slow rise
beneath a sky too quiet for lies,
took to the shore with rods in hand,
and left their words back on the land.
No need for vows or clever speech,
just tackle boxes within reach.
The water spoke in gentle sways,
and told their truths in each tidal phrase.
The first one cast with practiced grace,
a steady calm carved on his face.
The second whistled low and light,
his laugh a lantern in the night.
The third, a boy not far from grown,
felt less adrift when not alone.
No lectures given, none required:
just line and hook and shoulders tired.
The silence swelled with sacred weight,
a thousand things they'd never state.
Grief and joy and pride and scars
bobbing gently between the stars.
They didn't ask. They didn't pry.
They watched the silver minnows fly.
And when the sun began to dip,
they cracked a beer, they let it slip.
That this was church, without the pews.
That this was love, but dressed in blues.
That brotherhood is often found
in patience cast from solid ground.
And though they'd speak of bait and tide,
they knew what pulled them all inside:
a chance to mend, to just exist—
three men, one boat,
and nothing missed.

WIDOW

He was the echo in her laugh,
the steady hand that drew her back
from ledges built of long, hard soil
and winds that breathed of battle.
She wore his flannel like armor,
smelled the pine still stitched in its thread.
The house they built was small but held
a sky's worth of their silence.
Each morning rose with his old boots
beside the door—untouched, upright
as though he'd only gone to fetch
a fencepost or a song.
She doesn't pray, not with her hands,
but with the way she rides alone,
watching for his shadow
in the sway of distant cattle.
No stone could tell their story right.
No grave could hold her tether.
He is her very breath in gunfire,
her calm when storms refuse to sever.
Love like theirs don't bow to death
it kicks, it cusses, it burns the cold.
What once was held in mortal flesh
now rides the wind, unshaken, untold.

THERE WILL BE A PARTY

When you fall,
libations will pour,
songs will rise,
feet will flash across the floor,
bodies will meet,
debts will vanish–
love made,
mortgages erased.

When you fall,
there will be a party.

EXIT, PURSUED BY A NATURAL PREDATOR

I wore my youth like a borrowed flame,
Untouched by time, untouched by name.
But then footsteps came that I couldn't see.
Not fear, not man, just history.
He doesn't chase, he walks beside,
With ticking breath and patient stride.
My skin recalls what mirrors hide
That beauty shifts but doesn't slide.
I've lost the spark, not the command.
My voice still moves, my heart still stands.
He takes the bloom, not root or fire
My age a crown, not funeral pyre.
So let him come, I feel no shame.
Exit, yes–but still my name.

I DIDN'T KNOW I WAS TALKING TO A LADY

He tipped his hat like dust off a deal,
Voice like gravel and a boot full of steel.
Said, "Darlin', tell me what the night might buy–
A taste of heat or a whisperin' sigh?"
She turned slow, lips lined with fight,
Eyes like lanterns cuttin' through night.
"You askin' what a woman's worth in gold?
You better mind how your story's told."
He grinned like a gambler cocky of his hand,
Leaned on a lie like it helped him stand.
"Ain't no offense, just weighin' the cost.
A rose in the alley still knows she's lost."
"A rose?" she spat. "You mean a weed in the rain.
You talk like coin can pardon pain.
But some of us bloom just fine in the dirt,
Don't mean we're yours 'cause we wear the hurt."
He shrugged, lit a match on a sigh,
Didn't blink, didn't justify.
"Just askin' what the trade might be.
A drink, a bed, a night, or three."
"Trade?" she snapped. "You call this fair?
To weigh my worth on a barkeep's dare?"
She stood like a knife that hadn't been drawn,
But the duel was dull, and the moment gone.
He nodded once, and turned his gaze,
No shame, no need for truth or praise.
"Didn't know I was talkin' to a lady," he said.
Then walked on slow, like the words were dead.
Her price? Unknown. His aim? Unclear.
But the air between them stayed austere.

Like smoke from a gun that never fired
A dance begun, but not desired.

BLESSED ARE THE PIECE MAKERS

They came with hands like ash and fire,
Shaping thunder out of wire,
Carving breath where none belonged,
the silent saints who forged the song.
Not prayers, but powder kissed the sky,
And sermons spoke in howlers' cry.
The gospel here was flint and steel,
The hymn: a hammer's click made real.
Coins could buy a loaf or lie,
A warm bed, or a whispered sigh,
But iron spoke in clearer terms–
A standoff ends what justice blurred.
The ones who etched the spiral dance
Inside each chamber weren't by chance
Just smiths–they were the lords of peace,
Though what they gave was no release.
Their temples forged in burning red,
Where barrels bloomed and mercy bled.
They stitched no quilts, they sowed no seed,
But fed the wolves that laws would breed.
A man with gold might own the day,
But dusk belonged to those who'd spray
The dusk with lead, not lullabies.
The West was won by sharper cries.
And so they knelt not at a cross,
But workbenches of gain and loss.
For in a land where law was thin,
A piece in hand was peace within.

PART II
BLOOD AND DUST

A FISHER OF MEN?

He wore the collar like a badge,
but stained it with every swallow.
Said the Lord walks through the valley,
but he rode in on a borrowed hollow.
Quoting Psalms with a pistol's breath,
his sermon cracked like a busted tooth.
He preached of Eden, of brimstone, of death,
but never told the whole damn truth.
Some men bleed wine to feel the light,
some just drink 'cause they can't sleep nights.
One hand on the Book, one hand in sin,
does that make him beast or next of kin?
He said, *"Come follow, I'll make you fishers."*
But that line bent with liquor twitches.
A net full of doubt, no catch in sight,
just prayers washed down during bar room fights.
Don't judge too quick, that's fair to say,
but don't trust every man who prays.
Some wear the cloth to dodge the blame,
some wear it 'cause they fear their name.
He once was clean, or so he swears.
Now grace comes wrapped in muddied airs.
And maybe God still calls the flawed,
but does He whisper through applause?
A shepherd lost in a flock of none,
still yelling like the job ain't done.
So ask yourself when he starts to speak:
Is it God you hear,
Or a man too weak?

BLOOD FEUD

It started with a fence post split in spite,
a line drawn crooked under moonlight.
Two names carved deep in cypress bark:
both proud, both cruel, both born with dark.
Their fathers' fathers traded skin for coin,
built mansions on the lash's groin.
One bred cotton, the other bred fear;
neither could stand the other near.
A horse went missing. A field was burned.
A whip swung wild when backs were turned.
They called it theft, they called it war–
but what they wanted was something more.
Each son was taught with rifle in hand,
that honor don't bow, and blood must stand.
At balls, they danced in separate rooms
and sent each other sharpened tombs.
Plantation gates stayed chained with spite,
their pews split left and pews split right.
Even Sunday held no truce,
they'd rather pray in worn-out boots.
The war came down like fire from sky,
but even that could not untie
the red that ran from father to son
by war's end, both lost but had none.
Now moss hangs thick where names were sworn,
and children play where fields were torn.
A feud like this don't end with fate,
yet still, the air hums low with hate.
It ends when pride no longer feeds
on ghosts who whisper through the reeds.
But pride, like blood, is hard to kill
and vengeance grows where land stays still.

KNEW BORDEAUX

Head cradled in arms,
he preached as blood kissed the stones–
faith walks without fear.

THE BIG HOUSE ON FLAVIAN

Velvet curtains drawn like secrets untold,
Marble floors whisper sins in veins of gold.
A chandelier swinging with the weight of its lies,
And laughter echoes where innocence dies.
Gentlemen toast with imported deceit,
While barefoot boys wipe blood off the suite.
Every glass clinks with a contract signed,
And the wine's too red to deny the crime.
He speaks Italian but trades in flesh,
A serpent in silk with a saint's caress.
The parlor glows, the garden's trimmed,
But even flowers know what's buried within.
That city shines like a sinner's grin,
Piano tunes drown the ache of sin.
Deals done all quiet on cobbled walks,
While choirboys flinch at the sound of knocks.
What's power but a key to the cage you built?
A throne wrapped tight in a tapestry of guilt.
They say his house is the crown of the street,
But crowns draw flies when they're soaked in meat.
He don't run 'cause fear's a game he owns,
Where mothers weep and fathers groan.
And still the mayor dines like all is calm,
While the Devil plays host with an open palm.
No name on the door, but they all know the place,
Where truth gets traded for a silk-laced face.
It ain't just crime—it's legacy's kiss,
A kingdom of rot dressed up like bliss.
So tell me: Who guards the garden gate
When the serpent serves the wine on a silver plate?
And if ghosts walk Flavian after dark,
It's 'cause the big house was hell from the start.

I'M YOUR HUCKLEBERRY

Used to ride for the thrill, not a cause or a creed,
Just smoke in the lungs and a hunger to feed.
Steel on the hip, heart sealed in the shell,
Learned young that the West don't teach, it tells.
A dog with no chain, but its leash was fate,
Ran wild through the dusk, 'til the dusk got late.
Truth grew quiet when the gun got loud,
And pain learned to dance in a lawless crowd.
Called a killer, a drifter, a shadow in boots,
With roots in dust and disputes for loot.
But time don't flinch. It breaks, it bends.
It turns outlaws into tired old men.
Then a boy said "*Pa*," and the world stood still,
And love sliced through his urge to kill.
A woman held strong where the whiskey failed,
And silence weighed more than the jails he bailed.
No sermons, just scars that whispered change,
No preacher—just a promise, rearranged.
He ain't speak much, but when he did, it stayed,
Truth in the gravel, wisdom in the blade.
Built a home with calloused hands, not schemes,
Tried to scrub the blood from his in-between dreams.
Tilled that land like he once tilled fear,
And prayed to a sky that don't always hear.
So if you see him, his hat low and eyes like stone,
Know the fire's still there—but the war's his own.
He ain't perfect, but he's tried, and bled,
Trading wanted signs for a life instead.
He ain't your hero, just a man who knew
Sometimes dying right means living true.
And if the world comes knockin', full of worry
He'll spit, cock back, and say: *"Outta the damn way!"*

AIN'T NO RULES IN WAR, MISTER

1. **Shoot first when the sun is low,**
   Ride hard, leave quiet, move like a shadow.
2. **Trust no man who smiles too wide,**
   He'll shake your hand while your brother dies.
3. **Hide your steel, but keep it near,**
   A clean gun speaks when the law won't hear.
4. **Burn the trail and salt the ground,**
   Dead men talk when the crows come 'round.
5. **Spare no soul that draws on you,**
   Mercy's short and lead is true.
6. **Bury gold but not regret,**
   Both come back when the sun has set.
7. **Don't write your name on things you steal,**
   The grave don't care if the deed was real.
8. **A horse don't lie and neither does blood,**
   Follow both when the trail turns mud.
9. **Women watch more than they say,**
   Don't play games you can't outplay.
10. **When war begins, it don't stay clean,**
    You'll lose your soul before your spleen.

Ain't no rules in war, mister, just fate with teeth.
The only law you need is what's beneath.

PEELING MANGOES IN TAHITI

Peeling mangoes in the ocean's grin,
Skin sweet, sun thick, salt on skin.
Left the smoke where the rifles jam,
Now I tan where the tide don't give a damn.
Ain't no law but the breeze and sand,
No more maps, just lines in hand.
I used to **plan** heists with a cold cigar,
Now I **plan** naps under Southern stars.
Back then, **Plan A** was survive the dust,
Plan B was trust the one you must.
Now it's breakfast slow, barefoot grace,
Gold in the fruit, not a pistol's case.
They talk war—I sip rum, unbothered.
They plant flags—I just plant in water.
Let the suits **plan** railroads and bleed for land,
I **plan** for shade like a rich man can.
Used to break banks, now I break the rind
With juice on my fingers and peace in my mind.
No telegrams, no wires to scan,
Just mango flesh and a five-year **plan**.
I've seen death dance in a smoky hall,
Now birds sing plans with no plan at all.
Let the world chase what it never catches.
I **planned** my exit in fire and ashes.
So if they ask where the outlaw ran,
Tell 'em he's peeling mangoes, no need for a **plan**.

DICTATORS FALL

Like a curveball, sharp from twelve to six.
Then their heads roll,
knuckling through history's pitch.

LAST BOY

He sat at the train station, counting the Eagles that didn't perch and the years he didn't return.

YOU DON'T HIRE A SAINT TO CATCH A SINNER

Preachin' peace don't breach no gate,
Sinners slidin' while you meditate.
Ain't no hymn gon' halt that hustle,
Truth don't win when you flex no muscle.
Saints play clean—game gets dirtier,
Crooks move fast, saints move wordier.
Catchin' heat? You need the flame,
Saints point fingers, but sinners take aim.
Can't wear wings in a war-zone fight.
You need a shadow that moves at night.
You don't hire a saint to catch a sinner.
You play for keeps if you play for a winner.

PEARSON MATH

1 JR = 1 S + 1 SJ

Where:
- **JR** = Jack Rabbit
- **S** = Bowl of Soup
- **SJ** = Scout Jacket

WHO ARE THESE GD CREEPS?

Times are tough.
We're going to be okay.
Maybe not tomorrow–
Maybe not today.
Truth is:
Times are tough.
We're going to be okay.
Even if it feels off to you,
We're going to be okay.
Maybe not tomorrow–
Maybe not today.
Maybe.

PART III
LAW, LOSS, AND LEGACY

RATTUS RATTUS

Loyalty runs deep. "*Loyal to the soil*," we used to say. But betrayal has a boomerang's curve; it always finds its way back. We told ourselves nature could be outmaneuvered, but the truth is, we invited the storm. Trouble didn't come looking—we set the table for it. A hot shower turns cold, and so do people. Family ties, once solid, begin to swell and crack like old floorboards in floodwater. Some gave false names to survive. Others gave real ones to disappear. And how it all unraveled? It's a long story. Too long for one breath. Too short for forgiveness.

LEGAL WORK

Here it is, a groove slightly grim and alert,
Vest on tight and I'm dressed for the dirt.
Clock in my holster, I'm movin' like wind,
Ain't chasin' clout–just folks who ain't been.
Skip town? Then I'm the name that they curse,
Reading off warrants like a nurse with a purse.
Lurkin' in a Dodge, windows tinted for shade,
Knockin' on doors with a bounty to be paid.
No cape on my back, this ain't for glory,
Just legal work–not some bedtime story.
Cuffed in the ride, they askin' what's next,
But I just quote code, clean, calm, and direct.

See, folks skip court and vanish like mist,
'Til I pop up with a name on my list.
Don't run 'cause my shoes ain't built to lose,
I serve with respect, but I lace up my boots.
See the tool? It ain't gold, it's grit,
Earned on late nights when the trail don't quit.
Some talk rough, but they don't step near it,
This job ain't hype, you gotta move with spirit.
From bayous to streets, I stay in pursuit,
Legal, not lethal–but my methods astute.
I knock like the law, not a knock for fame,
Just a bounty, a signature, and a government name.
So next time you dip and think you ghost,
Remember there's one who don't do boasts.
Legal work, yeah, it don't always gleam,
But justice rides quiet with a steely-eyed team.

EVOLVE

They knew me in border towns by gun smoke and gin,
Card shark in the dark with a crooked grin.
Had a name folks whisper through teeth and lace,
Like I'd inked my sins on the sheriff's face.
Rail dust on my boots, and blood in my boots,
Every deal I struck wore tailored truths.
Some called it grit, some called it gall,
But I knew the weight behind each brawl.
The Lord stayed quiet but the dice would speak,
And the devil dealt hands imbued with hate.
I'd preach to the whores like I'd read their Psalms,
While I dug through their coffers with filthy palms.
Wasn't born bad, but I learned it quick,
'Fore the crops gave out and the land turned sick.
Ma wept prayers while the well ran dry,
And I learned how to steal with a thank-you-why.
Then one cold dusk in a brothel town,
I met a girl with a voice like down.
Told me her father once rode with Boone,
She smelled like redemption and silver spoon.
She bore my child 'neath a blood-washed moon,
Said, "*He'll never walk with a gun or rune.*"
I laughed, but that night I buried my Colt,
Next to my pride, with a flask and a jolt.
Now I shoe horses and mend split rails,
Read my son tales of the old gun trails.
He points to the villain and asks me, "*Pa?*"
And I lie like a saint with a wooden jaw.
But the lie's a prayer, and the prayer's a vow,
I bend each day to the yoke somehow.
Elvolve–see, it ain't just spelled wrong,
It's the path of a man when the nights feel long.
I'm still wanted, but now by a name,
By a boy who believes I am more than shame.
No bounty, no blood–just breakfast at dawn,
And a hope I'll pass like a law well drawn.

CALL THEM NOW

You call them.

Let them know:
The filth must go.
It must be burned,
It must be bled,
Like rot from the hearts
Of the half-living dead.
The filth must be cleansed.
No delay, no vow.
Call them then.
Or better: call them now.
Or wait.
Let time curdle slower.
From the gut of the gator,
Let judgment lower.

I'M HAPPY TO HELP A LITTLE

Sharper than judgment,
The blade finds its path.
You don't do wrong
And escape the aftermath.
You don't do bad things
And earn a good life.
Balance is settled
By deed or by grave.

OPEN WORLDS

Enjoy them.
I insist.

AN OUTLAW SHAPED BY AIR AND FIRE

She rode alone before they let her,
Wounds still warm, eyes like weather.
Didn't beg for space—she took it clean,
Like sky stretched wide on prairie lean.
A storm in lace, mended steel,
Too cold to break, too raw to heal.
She spoke in bullets, not in pleas,
Her freedom whispered through the trees.
You call her wild, she calls it her truth.
She watched the world hang dreams from roofs.
No god. No man. No final plan,
Just lawless stars and bloodied hands.
She ain't your damsel, ain't your muse,
She burns the script you dare to use.
Detached, yet loyal. Sharp, not sweet,
A hurricane with steady feet.
And when she leaves, she leaves like wind,
No final word. No tethered end.
Just a ghost in boots and leather smoke,
An air sign who refused the yoke.

YOU AYE PEE

Beneath a cloak of midnight sky,
Where the river's whisper wanders by,
Three watchers drifted, still and deep,
While stars above began to sweep.

A flame appeared—no hearth, no spark,
It danced across the heavens dark.
It flared, then withdrew, and soared once more,
A ghastly light from distant shore.

For hours it moved, both swift and wide,
As if some ship in space did glide.
No oar was touched, no sail was flown,
Yet they were not where they had known.

The boat had climbed the river's bend,
As if by will the light did send.
No dream it was, they did not sleep,
But truth too strange, and silence deep.

Long years before the world would claim
Such alien lights without voice or name,
It came, and passed, without a sound,
A mystery that still resounds.

THE GREEN CLAN

This here's dedicated …
To the smoke,
The fire,
And the lead–
WITH A GRIN!
Cowards!

A CRINE MAN

Jakey lay in the white snow, ribs cracked like old porch boards, breath hissing soft through blood-slick teeth. The sky above him was dull with smoke, the sun a boiled egg in a pan of ash. They laughed nearby–sharp, rusted sounds that caught in his ear like fishhooks.

His hand twitched toward the revolver just out of reach. Not for them. For her. For his wife. But he knew it wouldn't matter.

He was a crine man, he thought–once a fool in love, now a fool in death. Not a cryin' man, no, but a crine one: thinned by time and toil, worn sharp by regrets he never spoke aloud. He tasted the dust of his own undoing and whispered her name, barely a breath: *Sa–*

Was she safe? Did she have the rifle close? Did she bar the door? Did she know he'd die thinkin' only of her? Would she burn the world down after this, or fold into it like loincloth?

He blinked at the clouds, wondering if heaven was real or if it was just another promise sold cheap like horses and moonshine.

The last thing he felt wasn't the bullet. It was the wind shift. It was the smell of pine and fire, and the hollow ache of never gettin' to say goodbye.

They took his breath. Eventually, she took it back.

WIDOW II

What kind of woman shells the wheat,
then breaks the man who burned her seat?
Who traded apron strings for hot lead,
when smoke still clung to her homestead?
What kind of prayer is curled inside a fist,
with blood for balm, and no one missed?
Who kissed the ground where he was slain,
then rode that grief like driving rain?
What kind of vow survives the flame,
and calls the reaper by her name?
Who cuts her hair with sharpened glass,
and learns that mercy doesn't last?
What kind of scream don't beg or plead,
but stalks the hand that planted the seed?
Who once baked bread and stitched a seam,
but now kills silence in a scream?
What kind of fire won't wait for men,
or ask permission to begin?
Who jaunts like thunder through regret,
and shoots so she will not forget?
What kind of spine won't bend or yield,
but trades the cradle for the field?
Who buries softness, steels her grace,
a bullet's whisper in her place?
What kind of woman won't be tamed,
whose rage, not shame, is what she claimed?
She was a wife, but now? Beware:
She's carved her freedom from despair.

RED ONE

Seventeen carriages
ride the Southwestern Railroad loop.
Some bear livestock
destined for stew,
or Saint Denis prime rib,
or Preacher's Pride boots.

Others haul oil,
fueling the lamps of enlightenment,
as steel pipes rattle
toward lawmen's traps
with bureaucratic excitement.

Bolts of textile roll
ahead to markets far and wide,
and gravel-filled cars
bind worst to best,
laying roads to the east
while burying the West.

Seventeen carriages–
the longest train in the game.
Hauling the bones of land and labor,
agriculture and ore.
You'll wait a while to see it,
but the sight is worth far more.

PART IV
REDEMPTION AND RUIN

I'M LOOKING FOR A DISCOURAGED MAN

I'm not exactly in the market for melancholy company. Truth is, I've got plans involving stagecoaches–specifically, relieving them of their burdens. What I need from you is a bit of quiet intelligence: their routes, their schedules. And I'd prefer if the upstanding folks around here stayed none the wiser.

LAMB'S HEART

Hard pass. Arthur and John deserve better.

GODFORSAKEN MONEY LENDER

Ruiner of lives–
A widower's prize.
You wear debt like a crown
and feast as they drown.
Interest stacked high,
Hope left to die.
You built your throne
on broken homes.
Cursed every breath you loan–
Take your wretched self back home.
Hell awaits with an open gate
where vultures like you congregate.

HEREBY

I'm a gunsmith's dream, fleeing scenes as bodies swing.
Six-round capacity for shopkeepers and their wares, things
I'm after assets, currency, plus I'm that mean.
Black leather like I'm Dutch—with plans, dreams.
Stolen jewels from those who won't cherish the gleam.

I'm on the run, dodging bullets is my life's theme.
My bounty's S-tier, manipulating all peers.
Documenting frontiers, recruiting volunteers.
You can't catch me, baby, I'm made of gingerbread.
I'll cut a deal with feds, so much for that price on my head.

SAINT DENIS BY GASLIGHT

Who knows what kind of fairy a Mary is with lace and plea,
Spoke of love with a tremble, then dipped out clean on me.
She said, "*Help my kin*," like I was owed her history,
Then vanished in a prayer while I drowned in misery.

NAW, HE WAS BIGGER

Trigger-pullin' truth-teller, saddle-scarred lone rider,
Varmint-rippin' vulture, bounty-huntin' ghost glider.
Smoke-cloud breather, dead-eye bleeder,
Train-track terror, fast-draw heater.
Moonlit lurker, poker-faced sermon speaker,
Whiskey-mouth prophet, black-hat preacher.
Law-dodgin' drifter, coughin' through the silence,
Bandana-blood brother, baptized in violence.
Campfire thinker, debt-collectin' enforcer,
Graveyard whisperer, dusk's dark sorcerer.
Horseback humbler, tithes paid in sorrow,
One-way ticket to a breathless tomorrow.
Truth-wrestler, past-life penance bringer,
Steel-nerved strangler, Colt .45 singer.
Guilt-haunted, fate-taunted,
By the riverbank he stood, unloved but wanted.
Wolf-hearted letter writer, pain-sworn protector,
Hands of redemption, eyes of a specter.
No name spoken, just that sound of the wind,
He ain't comin' back–but he's always been.

CON JOB DRIP

Con job drip, old man slick
Gold watch tick, got a plan real quick
Stagecoach tip, got the whole crew rich
White hair wave, but the brain still lit
Talk sweet game, he ain't gotta draw sticks
Outlaw charm, turn a lawman snitch
Snake oil sold, now he ghost in the mist
Two-step clean, but he live in the grift
(Drip)

Slick tongue preacher, map plot teacher
Card sharp shuffle, yeah the mark never reach ya
Schemes so tight, you would think it was a feature
Smile so warm, but he colder than a freezer
Train job thinker, calm shot caller
Got Dutch dreamin' like the boy's his father
Smoke in his chest, still stand like a scholar
Even on the run, he got grace, got honor
(Woo!)

Dandy with the moves, he finesse that law
Manners like silk, but the game too raw
Talk his way out when the plan go south
And still got cash in the saddle and mouth
Who need a gun when the words hit slick?
Dress like a gent, but robs you quick
Con drip heavy, yeah, the style too rare
Old man calm, but he always prepared
Legacy built in the shadow and dust
Every big score got his mind and his trust
Ain't no rookie, that's the man with the gift
Put respect on the name when you talk that drip.
(Hey!)

BEAST FABLE

Red for the blood I spill with grace,
Gold for the dream I still chase.
Black for the coats who shadow the plan,
Blue for the law, gun tight in their hand.

White for the lies that built their throne,
Gray like the dusk where I ride alone.
I paint fire, I sketch fate,
Each stroke a war, each breath too late.

I preach with a tongue dipped in steel,
A sermon for men who forgot how to feel.
Smoke curls like questions I never ask,
Truth wears a mask, and I wear the task.

Freedom ain't free 'cause it's fought, it's bought,
In campfire talks and gunpowder thought.
They call me mad, a ghost, a sin,
But I was a prophet before the end began.

No color's pure when the lines are blurred,
I spoke thunder, they heard not a word.
Judge me not by coin or creed,
But by the men I fed, the mouths I freed.

Red for the price on a rebel's head,
Gold for the words I should've left unsaid …

MULIER EST RUINA VIRI

She told them in a room that smelled of gin and wood polish, upstairs from the saloon where the piano never stopped playing. The men came with hands too clean for this town and voices that never rose, not even when they spoke of death. She thought: *These men don't gamble, they close ledgers.*

She didn't say yes, not at first. She let the silence bend and stretch, like the elastic of a garter too long worn. She poured them drinks with a practiced hand and watched the whiskey draw a ring on the wood like a slow noose.

She had seen things—cruel things that wore lace and whispered lies with promises tucked under gunmetal smiles. She had smiled back. She once believed in the warmth of firelight and tin cups, in songs sung low and hands that only trembled in kindness. But the fire turned cold, and the songs turned sour.

So she told them.

Not everything. Just enough. A direction. A house near the swamp with windows like dead eyes. A man with a voice too smooth and a woman who cried in her sleep. She left out the child. She was not heartless. Just tired.

When they left, she sat on the edge of her bed, knees drawn up, fingers raw from clutching nothing. The silence came back, heavier now. The piano downstairs played a tune she didn't know anymore.

And for the first time in a long time, she felt alone the right way, cleanly.

STRAWBERRY, 3 A.M.

Dear Dev Team, I wrote before, but you still haven't answered,
My draft sits half-done; my advisor's patience dismembered.
I've sunk into your world, your open sky, your dusty roads,
At night I chase your freedom; by day my thesis erodes.
I've logged hours, days, my life held in your coded creed,
The chapters wait unfinished, but your landscape stalks my need.
Don't say "just one more mission," I've heard it all before.
I trade pages for pistols, research for a digital war.
Oh, I love your craft. I really do. But I feel betrayed,
By pixels richer than my prose, my PhD delayed.
I need help now. Please rescue me from this endless roam.
Sincerely, A Scholar Stranded, forgetting what is home.

Dear Scholar, I meant to write sooner but the servers were live,
We've been fixing new bugs, updating content, hoping you'd survive.
I get it, your world pulls you deep. The code, the dust, the lore,
But your dissertation waits. Don't lose sight of what you swore.
I never meant to steal your nights or turn your study cold,
We design to escape, not to fracture dreams you hold.
Remember why you started: the question, hypothesis in hand.
That passion's still alive. Don't let it drown in our sandbox land.
We're grateful you explored your heart within our world displayed.
But promise me you'll press pause, reclaim the plans you made.
Your thesis needs you, more than our next release could say.
Wrap it up. Then log back in. This time on your terms, your way.
Best, The Dev Team—crafting worlds, but rooting for your real play.

THIS GAME OF OURS

This game rides with ghosts.
Like Tony,
it mourns old codes,
honor lost in dust.

BOOM B.A.P. 1907

She woke with the hens, dust on her hem,
Folded their shirts but dreamed past them.
He came with law books, voice full of grace,
Asked for her truth—not just her place.

Now she walks where she once served tea,
No apron, just lace and memory.
They say she rose from a lawyer's hand.
But she built that life with her own bare plans.

ARABIAN OR APPALOOSA

Rode out the stable with the sun to my back
Smell of blood in the breeze and rifle on my lap
Strawberry passin', I ain't slowin' for no cart
Need a fast one with kick, not a mule with heart

Heard word of a trader got a steed on display
One's ghost-white slick, other's dappled with gray
Arabian or Appaloosa, don't care which one
Long as it run like sin and don't fear no gun

Bandana round my neck, coat *thicc* with dust
Lawmen watchin' close but in buckskin I trust
Slide through the fence line, my eyes on the prize
Ain't no sermon in my soul, just greedy skies

Campfire smoke curlin', smells like eat and sleep
Old man slumped with a map tucked deep
No honor in this, but I came for the loot
Put two in the dirt then I'm snatchin' that brute

Appaloosa kickin', but the Arab look clean
Mane like silk, eyes cruel and mean
Picked the reins up, and I vanished like breath
'Til I heard that badge holler, voice thick with death

Valentine's gate glintin', thought I'd made it whole
Then a shotgun barked and it swallowed my soul
Hit the ground rollin', blood drippin' like rain
Now I'm chained in a cell with a face full of shame

Sheriff spit near my boot, said, "We knew you'd lose, man"
For a damn horse?

Damn.

THE GREATEST GAME I'VE EVER PLAYED

The rest don't come close.
I tried to put my friends on.
They take my words as a joke:

"Ain't no way, bruh; surely you jest."

Thus, my words die slowly,
just like the Wild West.

They go on with their day
as I go on with mine,
imbued with cinematic literature,
with theory defined.

Perhaps it's an acquired taste,
like cilantro or emu.
This software is bespoke;
their games are from Temu.

Fine, don't take my word for it.
See if I care.
It's the greatest game I've ever played.
Wish you were here.

ACKNOWLEDGMENTS

With deep gratitude, I extend heartfelt thanks to the individuals who have played vital roles in the creation and support of *The Big House on Flavian*.

To **Paula Harrison-Hill**, thank you for being the personification of love and unwavering support. Your belief in me and your ability to see value in my voice has meant more than words can express.

To the incredible team at **Warren Publishing**, especially **Mindy Kuhn**, **Amy Ashby**, and **Lacey Cope**, thank you for your kindness, patience, and commitment to bringing my works to life. Your guidance and care throughout this process have been invaluable.

To **Hannah Cohen**, a brilliant poet and editor, thank you for lending your expertise to this work and for recognizing the beauty in *The Big House on Flavian*. Your insight and attention elevated every page.

To **Alexia McCarter**, the literal face of **Sole Food Brand**®, thank you for your friendship, belief in me, and deep investment in both myself and everything SFB represents. You are a cornerstone of this journey.

I am eternally grateful for the countless supporters of **Sole Food**®. In particular, I wish to thank **Dr. Pamela Richardson-Wilks, Dr. Willis Walter, Jonas Pope IV, Kenneth Holt, Bernard Bazemore, Shalon Sharpe, Mikel Brabham, David McMullin Jr.,** and **Nicholas Birdsong** for their GARGANTUAN financial support. Your generosity has not only sustained this brand, it has propelled it forward.

A special acknowledgment to **Chiniqua Radford** and **Dr. Tore Olsson**, my fellow *Red Dead Redemption 2* riders. Thank you for your camaraderie, enthusiasm, and unwavering support of *The Big House on Flavian*. You've made the journey all the more enjoyable.

To all who have believed in me, thank you. This book—and every word in it—is possible because of you.

FROM COLTER TO TEXT

This work is a love letter to what I consider a joyous experience: playing *Red Dead Redemption 2*.

When *RDR2* was released, I was finishing a PhD. I remember seeing a few commercials during that time, but I was unmoved and unbothered. Eight years earlier, I had played *Red Dead Redemption*, and at the time, it was the greatest game I had ever experienced. But during post-graduate school, gaming became a distant memory. When I finally played *Red Dead Redemption 2* in August 2023, I completed the story mode in four days. I didn't know those four days would serve as an invocation to a muse, one that would later inspire *The Big House on Flavian*.

This book documents my experience playing *Red Dead Redemption 2* and pays homage to Hip-Hop and popular culture while incorporating themes from the game. Readers familiar with Hip-Hop will recognize tributes intricately---and sometimes-- boldly woven into the text. For lovers of literature, *RDR2* is that and more. For those looking to understand America and her history, the game is an educational appetizer. It offers insight into the fall of the Old South, the Wild West, the rise of American industry, Civil Rights, Women's Suffrage, and political corruption.

Much like my book *Sole Food: Digestible Sneaker Culture*, this work introduces a cultural experience to communities who may not typically subscribe to poetry and celebrates the kindred spirits of those who do. Poetry itself is niche in concept, yet it has the power to reach everyone.

Simply put, *The Big House on Flavian* is love expressed. It is the joy of play, the depth of story, and the beauty of language transformed from Colter to text.

www.ingramcontent.com/pod-product-compliance
Lightning Source LLC
Chambersburg PA
CBHW030005050426
42451CB00006B/118